The Best Vegan Cookbook

Delicious Recipes for Plant-Based Diet

By Micha Potter

Sommario

Introduction

Vegetarianism as a lifestyle, in addition to respecting animals, can also bring other important health benefits such as a great reduction in the risk of diabetes and other diseases related to poor nutrition. in general, they choose to abolish all forms of meat including chicken, pork, beef, game and even fish. mainly there are two different strands, some taking their beliefs to the extreme, prefer to eliminate even products of animal origin and are called vegans, others who prefer to consume them anyway. At this point I invite you to consult our fantastic book and go in search of your favorite dish, bon appetit.

MAIN COURSE

Roasted Cauliflower and Garbanzo Beans

Ingredients

cooking

spray

1 tablespoon extra virgin olive

oil3 cloves garlic, minced

1/2 teaspoon sea salt

1/4 teaspoon ground black pepper3 1/2 cups sliced cauliflower

2 1/2 cups grape tomatoes

1 (15 ounce) can garbanzo beans, drained1 lime, cut into wedges

1 tablespoon chopped fresh cilantro

Preheat your oven to 450 degrees F.

Line a baking sheet with foil and grease with olive oil.Mix the olive oil, garlic, salt, and pepper in a bowl.

Add in the cauliflower, tomatoes, and garbanzo beansCombine until well coated.

Spread them out in a single layer on the baking sheet.Add the lime wedges.

Roast in the oven until vegetables become caramelized, for about 25minutes.

Take out the lime wedges and top with the cilantro.

Baked Smoky Broccoli and Garlic

Ingredients

cooking

spray

1 tablespoon extra virgin olive

oil3 cloves garlic, minced

1/2 teaspoon sea salt

1/4 teaspoon ground black pepper

½ tsp. cumin

½ tsp. annatto seeds

3 1/2 cups sliced
broccoli1 lime, cut into
wedges

1 tablespoon chopped fresh cilantro

Preheat your oven to 450 degrees F.

Line a baking sheet with foil and grease with olive oil.

Mix the olive oil, garlic, cumin, annatto seeds, salt, and
pepper in a bowl.

Add in the cauliflower, carrots, and
broccoliCombine until well coated.

Spread them out in a single layer on the baking
sheet.Add the lime wedges.

Roast in the oven until vegetables become caramelized, for
about 25minutes.

Take out the lime wedges and top with the cilantro.

Roasted Tomato Broccoli and Chickpeas

Ingredients

cooking

spray

1 tablespoon extra virgin olive

oil5 cloves garlic, minced

1/2 teaspoon sea salt

1/4 teaspoon ground black

pepper3 1/2 cups sliced broccoli

2 1/2 cups grape tomatoes

½ tsp. annatto seeds

½ cup green olives

½ cup capers

1 (15 ounce) can chick peas,

drained1 lime, cut into wedges

1 tablespoon chopped fresh cilantro

Preheat your oven to 450 degrees F.

Line a baking sheet with foil and grease with olive oil.

Mix the olive oil, garlic, annatto seeds, salt, and pepper in a bowl. Add in the broccoli, capers, olives, tomatoes, and garbanzo beansCombine until well coated.

Spread them out in a single layer on the baking sheet.Add the lime wedges.

Roast in the oven until vegetables become caramelized, for about 25minutes.

Take out the lime wedges and top with the cilantro.

Asian Roasted Broccoli and Choy Sum

Ingredients

cooking
spray

1 tablespoon sesame seed
oil3 cloves garlic, minced

1/2 teaspoon sea salt

1/4 teaspoon ground black pepper

3 1/2 cups sliced choy sum (Chinese Flowering
Cabbage)2 1/2 cups slice broccoli

1 tablespoon chopped fresh cilantro

Preheat your oven to 450 degrees F.

Line a baking sheet with foil and grease with
olive oil.Mix the sesame oil, garlic, salt, and
pepper in a bowl.Add in the choy sum and
broccoli

Combine until well coated.

Spread them out in a single layer on the baking sheet.

Roast in the oven until vegetables become caramelized, for about 25 minutes.

Top with the cilantro.

Roasted Soybean and Broccoli

Ingredients

cooking
spray

1 tablespoon extra virgin olive
oil3 cloves garlic, minced

1/2 teaspoon sea salt

1/4 teaspoon ground black
pepper3 1/2 cups sliced
cauliflower

2 1/2 cups cherry broccoli

1 (15 ounce) can soy beans,
drained1 tsp. cumin

1 tsp. dried annatto seeds

1 tablespoon chopped fresh cilantro

Preheat your oven to 450 degrees F.

Line a baking sheet with foil and grease with olive oil.Mix the olive oil, garlic, salt, and pepper in a bowl.

Add in the cauliflower, broccoli, and soy beansCombine until well coated.

Spread them out in a single layer on the baking sheet. Season with cumin. Annatto seeds and more salt if necessary.

Roast in the oven until vegetables become caramelized, for about 25minutes.

Take out the lime wedges and top with the cilantro.

Roasted Cauliflower and Lima Beans

Ingredients

cooking

spray

1 tablespoon melted vegan

butter/margarine9 cloves garlic, minced

1/2 teaspoon sea salt

1/4 teaspoon ground black

pepper1 1/2 cups sliced

cauliflower

3 1/2 cups cherry tomatoes

1 (15 ounce) can lima beans,

drained1 lemon , cut into wedges

Preheat your oven to 450 degrees F.

Line a baking sheet with foil and grease with melted vegan

butter ormargarine.

Mix the olive oil, garlic, salt, and pepper in a bowl. Add in the cauliflower, tomatoes, and lima beans Combine until well coated.

Spread them out in a single layer on the baking sheet. Add the lemon wedges.

Roast in the oven until vegetables become caramelized, for about 25 minutes.

Take out the lemon wedges.

Buttery Roasted Tomatoes and Edamame Beans

Ingredients

cooking

spray

1 tablespoon melted
butter8 cloves garlic,
minced

1/2 teaspoon sea salt

1/4 teaspoon Italian
seasoning3 1/2 cups sliced
cauliflower

2 1/2 cups cherry tomatoes

1 (15 ounce) can edamame beans,
drained1 lime, cut into wedges

¼ cup green olives

Preheat your oven to 450 degrees F.

Line a baking sheet with foil and grease with olive oil.

Mix the olive oil, garlic, salt, and Italian seasoning in a bowl.

Add in the cauliflower, green olives, tomatoes, and edamame
beansCombine until well coated.

Spread them out in a single layer on the baking

sheet. Add the lime wedges.

Roast in the oven until vegetables become caramelized, for about 25 minutes.

Take out the lime wedges and top with the cilantro.

Roasted Brussel Sprouts and Choy Sum

Ingredients

cooking

spray

1 tablespoon extra virgin olive

oil8 cloves garlic, minced

1/2 teaspoon sea salt

1/4 teaspoon rainbow

peppercorns3 1/2 cups sliced

choy sum

2 1/2 cups sliced brussel

sprouts1 lime, cut into wedges

1 tablespoon chopped fresh cilantro

Preheat your oven to 450 degrees F.

Line a baking sheet with foil and grease with olive

oil.Mix the olive oil, garlic, salt, and pepper in a

bowl.

Add in the choy sum and brussel sproutsCombine until well coated.

Spread them out in a single layer on the baking sheet.Add the lime wedges.

Roast in the oven until vegetables become caramelized, for about 25minutes.

Take out the lime wedges and top with the cilantro.

Roasted Choy Sum and Button Mushroom

Ingredients

cooking
spray

1 tablespoon sesame
oil3 cloves garlic,
minced 1/2 teaspoon
sea salt

1/4 teaspoon ground black
pepper3 1/2 cups sliced choy
sum

2 1/2 cups sliced button
mushrooms1 tablespoon chopped
fresh cilantro

Preheat your oven to 450 degrees F.

Line a baking sheet with foil and grease with sesame
oil.Mix the olive oil, garlic, salt, and pepper in a
bowl.

Add in the choy sum and button
mushroomsCombine until well coated.

Spread them out in a single layer on the baking
sheet.Add the lime wedges.

Roast in the oven until vegetables become caramelized, for
about 25minutes.

Top with the cilantro.

Thai Roasted Spicy Black Beans and Choy Sum

Ingredients

cooking
spray

1 tablespoon sesame
oil3 cloves garlic,
minced 1/2 teaspoon
sea salt

1 tbsp. Thai chili paste

1/4 teaspoon ground black pepper

3 1/2 cups Choy Sum, coarsely
chopped2 1/2 cups cherry tomatoes

1 (15 ounce) can black beans,
drained1 lime, cut into wedges

1 tablespoon chopped fresh cilantro

Preheat your oven to 450 degrees F.

Line a baking sheet with foil and grease with sesame oil.

Mix the olive oil, garlic, salt, Thai chili paste, and pepper in a bowl. Add in the choy sum, tomatoes, and black beans

Combine until well coated.

Spread them out in a single layer on the baking sheet. Add the lime wedges.

Roast in the oven until vegetables become caramelized, for about 25 minutes.

Take out the lime wedges and top with the cilantro.

Simple Roasted Mustard Greens

Ingredients

cooking
spray

1 tablespoon extra virgin olive
oil3 cloves garlic, minced

1/2 teaspoon sea salt

1/4 teaspoon ground black
pepper3 1/2 cups sliced
mustard greens 2 1/2 cups
cherry tomatoes

1 tablespoon chopped fresh thyme

Preheat your oven to 450 degrees F.

Line a baking sheet with foil and grease with olive
oil.Mix the olive oil, garlic, salt, and pepper in a
bowl.

Add in the mustard greens and tomatoesCombine until well coated.

Spread them out in a single layer on the baking sheet.

Roast in the oven until vegetables become caramelized, for about 25minutes.

Top with the thyme.

Simple Roasted Broccoli and Cauliflower

Ingredients

cooking
spray

1 tablespoon extra virgin olive
oil3 cloves garlic, minced

1/2 teaspoon sea salt

1/4 teaspoon ground black
pepper3 1/2 cups broccoli
florets

2 1/2 cups cauliflower florets

1 tablespoon chopped fresh thyme

Preheat your oven to 450 degrees F.

Line a baking sheet with foil and grease with olive
oil.Mix the olive oil, garlic, salt, and pepper in a
bowl.

Add in the cauliflower and
tomatoesCombine until well
coated.

Spread them out in a single layer on the baking sheet.

Roast in the oven until vegetables become caramelized, for
about 25minutes.

Top with the thyme.

Simple Roasted Mustard Greens and Red Cabbage

Ingredients

cooking spray

1 tablespoon extra virgin olive
oil1/2 teaspoon sea salt

1/4 teaspoon ground black pepper

Main Ingredients

1/4 lb. mustard greens

1/2 medium red cabbage, sliced thinly

Preheat your oven to 450 degrees F.

Line a baking sheet with foil and grease with olive oil. Mix the extra ingredients thoroughly.

Add in the main ingredientsCombine until well coated.

Spread them out in a single layer on the baking sheet.

Roast in the oven until vegetables become caramelized, for about 25 minutes.

Roasted Spinach and Mustard Greens

Ingredients

cooking spray

1 tablespoon extra virgin olive
oil1/2 teaspoon sea salt

1/4 teaspoon ground black pepper

Main Ingredients

1 bunch of mustard greens, rinsed and
drained1 bunch of spinach, rinsed and
drained

Preheat your oven to 450 degrees F.

Line a baking sheet with foil and grease with olive
oil.Mix the extra ingredients thoroughly.

Add in the main
ingredientsCombine until

well coated.

Spread them out in a single layer on the baking sheet.

Roast in the oven until vegetables become caramelized, for about 25 minutes.

Roasted Spinach and Artichoke Hearts

Ingredients
cooking spray

1 tablespoon extra virgin olive oil1/2 teaspoon sea salt

1/4 teaspoon ground black pepperMain Ingredients

1 bunch of spinach, rinsed and drained1 cup canned artichoke hearts

Preheat your oven to 450 degrees F.

Line a baking sheet with foil and grease with olive oil.Mix the extra ingredients thoroughly.

Add in the main ingredientsCombine until well coated.

Spread them out in a single layer on the baking sheet.

Roast in the oven until vegetables become caramelized, for about 25minutes.

Roasted Napa Cabbage and Turnips

Ingredients

cooking spray

1 tablespoon extra virgin olive oil 1/2 teaspoon sea salt

1/4 teaspoon ground black pepper

Main Ingredients

1/2 medium Napa cabbage, sliced thinly 1 medium turnip, sliced thinly

Preheat your oven to 450 degrees F.

Line a baking sheet with foil and grease with olive oil. Mix the extra ingredients thoroughly.

Add in the main ingredients Combine until well coated.

Spread them out in a single layer on the baking sheet.

Roast in the oven until vegetables become caramelized, for about 25 minutes.

Roasted Parsnips and Watercress

Ingredients

cooking spray

1 tablespoon extra virgin olive

oil1/2 teaspoon sea salt

1/4 teaspoon ground black pepper

Main Ingredients

1 medium parsnip, sliced thinly

1 bunch of watercress, rinsed and drained

Preheat your oven to 450 degrees F.

Line a baking sheet with foil and grease with olive

oil.Mix the extra ingredients thoroughly.

Add in the main

ingredientsCombine until

well coated.

Spread them out in a single layer on the baking sheet.

Roast in the oven until vegetables become caramelized, for about 25 minutes.

Simple Roasted Kale Artichoke Heart and Choy Sum

Ingredients

cooking spray

1 tablespoon extra virgin olive
oil1/2 teaspoon sea salt

1/4 teaspoon ground black pepper

Main Ingredients

1 bunch of kale, rinsed and
drained1 cup canned artichoke
hearts

1/2 medium Chinese flowery cabbage (choy sum), coarsely
chopped

Preheat your oven to 450 degrees F.

Line a baking sheet with foil and grease with olive
oil.Mix the extra ingredients thoroughly.

Add in the main
ingredientsCombine until
well coated.

Spread them out in a single layer on the baking sheet.

Roast in the oven until vegetables become caramelized, for
about 25minutes.

Roasted Napa Cabbage Baby Carrots and Watercress

Ingredients

cooking spray

1 tablespoon extra virgin olive

oil1/2 teaspoon sea salt

1/4 teaspoon ground black pepper

Main Ingredients

1/2 medium Napa cabbage, sliced
thinly5 baby carrots

1 bunch of watercress, rinsed and drained

Preheat your oven to 450 degrees F.

Line a baking sheet with foil and grease with olive
oil.Mix the extra ingredients thoroughly.

Add in the main
ingredientsCombine until
well coated.

Spread them out in a single layer on the baking sheet.

Roast in the oven until vegetables become caramelized, for
about 25minutes.

Roasted Spinach and Mustard Greens

Ingredients

cooking spray

1 tablespoon extra virgin olive
oil1/2 teaspoon sea salt

1/4 teaspoon ground black
pepperMain Ingredients

5 baby carrots

1 bunch of spinach, rinsed and drained

1 bunch of mustard greens, rinsed and drained

Preheat your oven to 450 degrees F.

Line a baking sheet with foil and grease with olive
oil.Mix the extra ingredients thoroughly.

Add in the main
ingredientsCombine until
well coated.

Spread them out in a single layer on the baking sheet.

Roast in the oven until vegetables become caramelized, for about 25 minutes.

Roasted Artichoke Hearts and Napa Cabbage

Ingredients

cooking spray

1 tablespoon extra virgin olive
oil1/2 teaspoon sea salt

1/4 teaspoon ground black
pepperMain Ingredients

1/2 medium napa cabbage, sliced
thinly1 cup canned artichoke hearts

Preheat your oven to 450 degrees F.

Line a baking sheet with foil and grease with olive
oil.Mix the extra ingredients thoroughly.

Add in the main
ingredientsCombine until
well coated.

Spread them out in a single layer on the baking sheet.

Roast in the oven until vegetables become caramelized, for about 25minutes.

Roasted Kale and Bok Choy

Ingredients

cooking spray

1 tablespoon extra virgin olive
oil1/2 teaspoon sea salt

1/4 teaspoon ground black
pepperMain Ingredients

1 bunch of kale, rinsed and drained

1 bunch of bok choy, rinsed ,drained and coarsely chopped

Preheat your oven to 450 degrees F.

Line a baking sheet with foil and grease with olive
oil.Mix the extra ingredients thoroughly.

Add in the main
ingredientsCombine until
well coated.

Spread them out in a single layer on the baking sheet.

Roast in the oven until vegetables become caramelized, for about 25minutes.

Roasted Spinach and Kale

Ingredients

cooking spray

1 tablespoon extra virgin olive
oil1/2 teaspoon sea salt

1/4 teaspoon ground black pepper

Main Ingredients

1 bunch of spinach, rinsed and
drained1 bunch of kale, rinsed and
drained

Preheat your oven to 450 degrees F.

Line a baking sheet with foil and grease with olive
oil.Mix the extra ingredients thoroughly.

Add in the main
ingredientsCombine until

well coated.

Spread them out in a single layer on the baking sheet.

Roast in the oven until vegetables become caramelized, for about 25minutes.

Roasted Lima Beans and Summer Squash

Ingredients

2 (15 ounce) cans lima beans, rinsed and drained

1/2 summer squash - peeled, seeded, and cut into 1-inch
pieces1 red onion, diced

1 sweet potato, peeled and cut into 1-inch
cubes2 large carrots, cut into 1 inch pieces

3 medium potatoes, cut into 1-inch
pieces3 tablespoons sesame oil

Seasoning
ingredients1
teaspoon salt

1/2 teaspoon ground black
pepper1 teaspoon onion powder

2 teaspoon garlic powder

1 teaspoon ground fennel

seeds1 teaspoon dried rubbed
sage Garnishing Ingredients

2 green onions, chopped (optional)

Preheat your oven to 350 degrees
F. Grease your baking pan.

Combine the beans, summer squash, onion, sweet potato,
carrots, and russet potatoes on the prepared sheet pan.

Drizzle with the oil and toss to coat.
Combine the seasoning ingredients in a
bowl

Sprinkle them over the vegetables on the pan and toss to coat
with seasonings.

Bake in the oven for 25 minutes.

Stir frequently until vegetables are soft and lightly
browned and beans are crisp, for about 20 to 25 minutes
more.

Season with more salt and black pepper to taste, top with the
green onion before serving.

Roasted Borlotti Bean and Summer Squash

Ingredients

2 (15 ounce) borlotti beans, rinsed and drained

1/2 summer squash - peeled, seeded, and cut into 1-inch pieces1 red onion, diced

1 sweet potato, peeled and cut into 1-inch

cubes2 large carrots, cut into 1 inch pieces

3 medium potatoes, cut into 1-inch
pieces3 tablespoons extra virgin oil

Seasoning
ingredients1
teaspoon salt

1/2 teaspoon ground black
pepper1 teaspoon onion powder

2 teaspoon garlic
powder1 teaspoon
cumin

1 teaspoon chili
powderGarnishing
Ingredients

2 green onions, chopped
(optional) Preheat your oven to
350 degrees F.Grease your
baking pan.

Combine the beans, squash, onion, sweet potato, carrots,
andpotatoes on the prepared sheet pan.

Drizzle with the oil and toss to coat.

Combine the seasoning ingredients in a
bowl

Sprinkle them over the vegetables on the pan and toss to coat
with seasonings.

Bake in the oven for 25 minutes.

Stir frequently until vegetables are soft and lightly
browned and beans are crisp, for about 20 to 25 minutes
more.

Season with more salt and black pepper to taste, top with the
green onion before serving.

Roasted Thai Artichoke Hearts and Broccoli

Ingredients

1 1/2 pounds broccoli, cut into
chunks2 tablespoons sesame seed
oil

10 cloves garlic, thinly
sliced1 tbsp. Thai chili
garlic paste

2 teaspoons chopped Fresh Thai
basil2 teaspoons sea salt

1 bunch artichoke hearts, trimmed and cut into 1 inch
piecesPreheat your oven to 425 degrees F.

In a baking pan, combine the first 5 ingredients and 1/2 of
the seasalt.

Cover with foil.

Bake 20 minutes in the oven.
Combine the broccoli, oil, and
salt.

Cover, and cook for about 15 minutes, or until the broccoli becomestender.

Increase your oven temperature to 450 degrees F.

Take out the foil, and cook for 8 minutes, until potatoes becomelightly browned.

Roasted Lemon Green Beans and Red Potatoes

Ingredients

1 1/2 pounds red potatoes, cut into
chunks2 tablespoons salted butter

12 cloves garlic, thinly
sliced1 tbsp. lemon juice

1 tsp. annatto
seeds2 teaspoons
sea salt

1 bunch green beans, trimmed and cut into 1 inch
piecesPreheat your oven to 425 degrees F.

In a baking pan, combine the first 5 ingredients and 1/2 of
the seasalt.

Cover with foil.

Bake 20 minutes in the oven.
Combine the asparagus, oil, and
salt.

Cover, and cook for about 15 minutes, or until the potatoes becomestender.

Increase your oven temperature to 450 degrees F.

Take out the foil, and cook for 8 minutes, until potatoes becomelightly browned.

Roasted Green Beans Carrots & Turnips

Ingredients

1/2 pound turnips, cut into chunks

½ pound carrots, cut into chunks

½ pound French green
beans2 tablespoons
sesame oil

10 cloves garlic, thinly sliced

1 tsp. Chinese 5 spice
powder2 teaspoons sea salt

1 bunch fresh asparagus, trimmed and cut into 1 inch
piecesPreheat your oven to 425 degrees F.

In a baking pan, combine the first 6 ingredients and 1/2 of
the seasalt.

Cover with foil.

Bake 20 minutes in the oven.
Combine the asparagus, oil, and

salt.

Cover, and cook for about 15 minutes, or until the French greenbeans becomes tender.

Increase your oven temperature to 450 degrees F.

Take out the foil, and cook for 8 minutes, until French green beansbecome lightly browned.

Roasted Italian Kohlrabi and Asparagus

Ingredients

1 1/2 pounds kohlrabi, cut into
chunks2 tablespoons extra virgin
olive oil

12 cloves garlic, thinly
sliced1 tsp. Italian
seasoning

4 teaspoons dried
thyme2 teaspoons sea
salt

1 bunch fresh asparagus, trimmed and cut into 1 inch
piecesPreheat your oven to 425 degrees F.

In a baking pan, combine the first 5 ingredients and 1/2 of
the seasalt.

Cover with foil.

Bake 20 minutes in the oven.
Combine the asparagus, oil, and

salt.

Cover, and cook for about 15 minutes, or until the kohlrabi becomestender.

Increase your oven temperature to 450 degrees F.

Take out the foil, and cook for 8 minutes, until kohlrabi become lightlybrowned.

Roasted Yucca Root and Kohlrabi

Ingredients

½ pound yucca root, cut into
chunks1/2 pounds kohlrabi, cut
into chunks2 tablespoons extra
virgin olive oil 12 cloves garlic,
thinly sliced

4 teaspoons Herbs de
Provence2 teaspoons sea salt

1 bunch fresh asparagus, trimmed and cut into 1 inch
piecesPreheat your oven to 425 degrees F.

In a baking pan, combine the first 6 ingredients and 1/2 of
the seasalt.

Cover with foil.

Bake 20 minutes in the oven.
Combine the asparagus, oil, and
salt.

Cover, and cook for about 15 minutes, or until the kohlrabi and yuccaroot becomes tender.

Increase your oven temperature to 450 degrees F.

Take out the foil, and cook for 8 minutes, until kohlrabi become lightlybrowned.

Roasted Yucca Root, Turnips & Carrots

Ingredients

1/2 pound carrots, cut into chunks

½ pound yucca root, cut into chunks

½ pound turnips, cut into
chunks 2 tablespoons extra
virgin olive oil12 cloves garlic,
thinly sliced

1 tbsp. and 1 tsp. dried
rosemary4 teaspoons dried
thyme

2 teaspoons sea salt

1 bunch fresh asparagus, trimmed and cut into 1 inch
piecesPreheat your oven to 425 degrees F.

In a baking pan, combine the first 7 ingredients and 1/2 of
the seasalt.

Cover with foil.

Bake 20 minutes in the oven.
Combine the asparagus, oil, and
salt.

Cover, and cook for about 15 minutes, or until the root
vegetablesbecomes tender.

Increase your oven temperature to 450 degrees F.

Take out the foil, and cook for 8 minutes, until yucca root
becomelightly browned.

Roasted Yucca Root and Beets

Ingredients

1/2 pounds beets, cut into chunks

½ pound yucca root, cut into chunks

½ pound turnips, cut into
chunks 2 tablespoons extra
virgin olive oil12 cloves garlic,
thinly sliced

1 tbsp. and 1 tsp. dried
rosemary4 teaspoons dried
thyme

2 teaspoons sea salt

1 bunch fresh asparagus, trimmed and cut into 1 inch
piecesPreheat your oven to 425 degrees F.

In a baking pan, combine the first 7 ingredients and 1/2 of
the sea salt.

Cover with foil.

Bake 20 minutes in the oven.

Combine the asparagus, oil, and

salt.

Cover, and cook for about 15 minutes, or until the root

vegetablesbecomes tender.

Increase your oven temperature to 450 degrees F.

Take out the foil, and cook for 8 minutes, until potatoes

becomelightly browned.

Roasted Nutty Potato and Sweet Potato

Ingredients

1/2 pounds red potatoes, cut into chunks

½ pound sweet potatoes, cut into
chunks2 tablespoons peanut oil

12 cloves garlic, thinly sliced

1 tbsp. and 1 tsp. herbs de
Provence2 teaspoons sea salt

1 bunch fresh asparagus, trimmed and cut into 1 inch pieces

Preheat your oven to 425 degrees F.

In a baking pan, combine the first 6 ingredients and 1/2 of
the seasalt.

Cover with foil.

Bake 20 minutes in the oven.
Combine the asparagus, oil, and

salt.

Cover, and cook for about 15 minutes, or until the root vegetablesbecomes tender.

Increase your oven temperature to 450 degrees F.

Take out the foil, and cook for 8 minutes, until potatoes becomelightly browned.

Roasted Kohlrabi and White Yam

Ingredients

1/2 pounds white yam, cut into chunks

½ pound kohlrabi, cut into chunks

½ pound purple yam, cut into
chunks2 tablespoons extra virgin
olive oil 12 cloves garlic, thinly
sliced

1 tbsp. and 1 tsp. dried
rosemary4 teaspoons dried
thyme

2 teaspoons sea salt

1 bunch fresh asparagus, trimmed and cut into 1 inch pieces

Preheat your oven to 425 degrees F.

In a baking pan, combine the first 7 ingredients and 1/2 of
the seasalt.

Cover with foil.

Bake 20 minutes in the oven.
Combine the asparagus, oil, and
salt.

Cover, and cook for about 15 minutes, or until the root
vegetablesbecomes tender.

Increase your oven temperature to 450 degrees F.

Take out the foil, and cook for 8 minutes, until potatoes
becomelightly browned.

Roasted Yams and Asparagus

Ingredients

1/2 pound purple yam, cut into chunks

½ pound white yam, cut into chunks

½ pound sweet potato

2 tablespoons canola olive
oil12 cloves garlic, thinly
sliced 2 tsp. Italian
seasoning

2 teaspoons sea salt

1 bunch fresh asparagus, trimmed and cut into 1 inch pieces

Preheat your oven to 425 degrees F.

In a baking pan, combine the first 6 ingredients and 1/2 of the seasalt.

Cover with foil.

Bake 20 minutes in the oven.

Combine the asparagus, oil, and
salt.

Cover, and cook for about 15 minutes, or until the root
vegetablesbecomes tender.

Increase your oven temperature to 450 degrees F.

Take out the foil, and cook for 8 minutes, until potatoes
becomelightly browned.

Baked Yucca Root Asparagus and Trunips

Ingredients

1 pound turnips, cut into chunks

½ pound parsnips, cut into chunks

½ pound yucca root

2 tablespoons extra virgin olive oil12 cloves garlic, thinly sliced

1 tbsp. and 1 tsp. dried rosemary4 teaspoons dried thyme

2 teaspoons sea salt

1 bunch fresh asparagus, trimmed and cut into 1 inch pieces

Preheat your oven to 425 degrees F.

In a baking pan, combine the first 7 ingredients and 1/2 of the seasalt.

Cover with foil.

Bake 20 minutes in the oven.

Combine the asparagus, olive oil, and salt.

Cover, and cook for about 15 minutes, or until the root vegetablesbecomes tender.

Increase your oven temperature to 450 degrees F.

Take out the foil, and cook for 8 minutes, until potatoes becomelightly browned.

Baked Kohlrabi Yucca Root and Mustard Greens

Ingredients

1/2 pound kohlrabi, cut into chunks

½ pound yucca root, cut into chunks

½ pound mustard greens

2 tablespoons extra virgin olive
oil12 cloves garlic, thinly sliced

1 tbsp. and 1 tsp. dried
rosemary4 teaspoons dried
thyme

2 teaspoons sea salt

1 bunch fresh green beans, trimmed and cut into 1 inch pieces

Preheat your oven to 425 degrees F.

In a baking pan, combine the first 7 ingredients and 1/2 of
the seasalt.

Cover with foil.

Bake 20 minutes in the oven.

Combine the green beans, olive oil, and salt.

Cover, and cook for about 15 minutes, or until the root vegetablesbecomes tender.

Increase your oven temperature to 450 degrees F.

Take out the foil, and cook for 8 minutes, until potatoes becomelightly browned.

Baked Broccoli Sprouts and Carrots

Ingredients

½ pound carrots, cut into chunks

½ pound brussels sprouts

½ pound Broccoli
sprouts 2 tablespoons
sesame oil

12 cloves garlic, thinly sliced

1 tbsp. and 1 tsp. ginger,
minced4 teaspoons spring
onions

2 teaspoons sea salt

1 bunch fresh asparagus, trimmed and cut into 1 inch pieces

Preheat your oven to 425 degrees F.

In a baking pan, combine the first 7 ingredients and 1/2 of the seasalt.

Cover with foil.

Bake 20 minutes in the oven.

Combine the asparagus, olive oil, and salt.

Cover, and cook for about 15 minutes, or until the carrots becomestender.

Increase your oven temperature to 450 degrees F.

Take out the foil, and cook for 8 minutes, until carrots become lightly browned.

Baked Brussel Sprouts & Red Onion Glazed with Balsamic Vinegar

Ingredients

1 (16 ounce) package fresh Brussels sprouts2 small red onions, thinly sliced

¼ cup and 1 tbsp. extra-virgin olive oil, divided1/4 teaspoon sea salt

1/4 teaspoon rainbow peppercorns1 shallot, chopped

1/4 cup balsamic vinegar

1 tablespoon chopped fresh rosemary

Preheat your oven to 425 degrees F (220 degrees C).Grease a baking pan.

Combine Brussels sprouts and onion in a bowl
Add 4 tablespoons olive oil, salt, and peppercorns

Toss to coat and spread the sprouts mixture on the pan.

Bake in the oven until sprouts and red onion become tender, forabout 25 to 30 minutes.

Heat the remaining tablespoon of olive oil in a small skillet overmedium-high heat

Sauté the shallots until tender, for about 5 minutes.

Add balsamic vinegar and cook until the glaze is reduced for about 5minutes.

Add rosemary into the balsamic glaze and pour over the sprouts.

Baked Cabbage and Red Onion

Ingredients

1 (16 ounce) package fresh green cabbage, quartered2 small red onions, thinly sliced

¼ cup and 1 tbsp. extra-virgin olive oil, divided1/4 teaspoon sea salt

1/4 teaspoon ground black peppercorns1 shallot, chopped

1/4 cup red wine vinegar

1 tablespoon chopped fresh rosemary

Preheat your oven to 425 degrees F (220 degrees C).Grease a baking pan.

Combine cabbage and onion in a bowl

Add 4 tablespoons olive oil, salt, and peppercorns

Toss to coat and spread the sprouts mixture on the pan.

Bake in the oven until sprouts and onion become tender, for about25 to 30 minutes.

Heat the remaining tablespoon of olive oil in a small skillet overmedium-high heat

Sauté the shallots until tender, for about 5 minutes.

Add vinegar and cook until the glaze is reduced for about 5 minutes.Add rosemary into the vinaigrette

Baked Purple Cabbage with Rainbow Peppercorns

Ingredients

1 (16 ounce) package fresh purple cabbage2 small red onions, thinly sliced

1/2 cup and 1 tbsp. extra-virgin olive oil, divided1/4 teaspoon sea salt

1/4 teaspoon rainbow peppercorns1 shallot, chopped

1/4 cup balsamic vinegar1 tsp. herbs de Provence

Preheat your oven to 425 degrees F (220 degrees C).Grease a baking pan.

Combine cabbage and onion in a bowl

Add 4 tablespoons olive oil, salt, and peppercorns

Toss to coat and spread the sprouts mixture on the pan.

Bake in the oven until sprouts and onion become tender, for about25 to 30 minutes.

Heat the remaining tablespoon of olive oil in a small skillet overmedium-high heat

Sauté the shallots until tender, for about 5 minutes.

Add balsamic vinegar and cook until the glaze is reduced for about 5minutes.

Add herbs de Provence into the balsamic glaze and pour over thesprouts.

Roasted Napa Cabbage with Red Onions

Ingredients

1 (16 ounce) package fresh Napa
cabbage2 small red onions, thinly sliced

¼ cup and 1 tbsp. extra-virgin olive oil,
divided1/4 teaspoon sea salt

1/4 teaspoon rainbow
peppercorns1 shallot, chopped

1/4 cup balsamic
vinegar1 tsp. Italian
seasoning

Preheat your oven to 425 degrees F (220 degrees
C).Grease a baking pan.

Combine cabbage and onion in a bowl

Add 4 tablespoons olive oil, salt, and peppercorns

Toss to coat and spread the sprouts mixture on the pan.

Bake in the oven until sprouts and onion become tender, for about25 to 30 minutes.

Heat the remaining tablespoon of olive oil in a small skillet overmedium-high heat

Sauté the shallots until tender, for about 5 minutes.

Add balsamic vinegar and cook until the glaze is reduced for about 5minutes.

Add Italian seasoning into the balsamic glaze and pour over thesprouts.

Roasted Savoy Cabbage and Vidalia Onion

Ingredients

2 Vidalia onions, thinly sliced

¼ cup and 1 tbsp. extra-virgin olive oil, divided1/4 teaspoon sea salt

1/4 teaspoon black peppercorns1 shallot, chopped

1/4 cup white wine vinegar

1 tablespoon chopped fresh rosemary

Preheat your oven to 425 degrees F (220 degrees C).Grease a baking pan.

Combine cabbage and onion in a bowl

Add 4 tablespoons olive oil, salt, and peppercorns

Toss to coat and spread the sprouts mixture on the pan.

Bake in the oven until sprouts and onion become tender, for about25 to 30 minutes.

Heat the remaining tablespoon of olive oil in a small skillet overmedium-high heat

Sauté the shallots until tender, for about 5 minutes.

Add white wine vinegar and cook until the glaze is reduced for about5 minutes.

Add rosemary into the balsamic glaze and pour over the sprouts.

Roasted Red Cabbage with Balsamic Glaze

Ingredients

1 (16 ounce) package fresh Red
Cabbage2 small red onions, thinly
sliced

¼ cup and 1 tbsp. extra-virgin olive oil,
divided1/4 teaspoon sea salt

1/4 teaspoon rainbow
peppercorns1 shallot, chopped

1/4 cup balsamic vinegar

1 tablespoon chopped fresh thyme

Preheat your oven to 425 degrees F (220 degrees
C).Grease a baking pan.

Combine cabbage and onion in a bowl

Add 4 tablespoons olive oil, salt, and peppercorns

Toss to coat and spread the sprouts mixture on the pan.

Bake in the oven until sprouts and onion become tender, for about25 to 30 minutes.

Heat the remaining tablespoon of olive oil in a small skillet overmedium-high heat

Sauté the shallots until tender, for about 5 minutes.

Add balsamic vinegar and cook until the glaze is reduced for about 5minutes.

Add thyme into the balsamic glaze and pour over the sprouts.

Baked Crimini Mushrooms and Red Potatoes

Ingredients

1 pound red potatoes, halved

2 tablespoons extra virgin olive
oil1/2 pound Cremini
mushrooms

8 cloves unpeeled garlic

2 tablespoons chopped fresh

thyme1 tablespoon extra-virgin
olive oil

sea salt and ground black pepper to
taste1/4 pound cherry tomatoes

3 tablespoons toasted pine
nuts1/4 pound spinach, thinly
sliced

Preheat your oven to 425 degrees
F.Spread the potatoes in a pan

Drizzle with 2 tablespoons of olive oil and roast for 15
minutesturning once.

Add the mushrooms with the stem sides up

Add the garlic cloves to pan and cook until lightly
brownedSprinkle with thyme.

Drizzle with 1 tablespoon olive oil and season with sea salt and
blackpepper.

Return to the oven and bake for 5
min.Add the cherry tomatoes to the

pan.

Return to oven and bake until mushrooms become softened, for 5min.

Sprinkle the pine nuts over the potatoes and mushrooms.Serve with the spinach.

Baked Crimini Mushrooms with Rutabaga

Ingredients

1 pound rutabaga, halved

2 tablespoons extra virgin olive oil1/2 pound cremini mushrooms

8 cloves unpeeled garlic

2 tablespoons chopped fresh thyme2 tablespoons extra-virgin olive oil

sea salt and ground black pepper to taste1/4 pound cherry tomatoes

3 tablespoons toasted walnuts 1/4 pound spinach, thinly sliced

Preheat your oven to 425 degrees

F. Spread the sweet potatoes in a
pan

Drizzle with 2 tablespoons of olive oil and roast for 15
minutesturning once.

Add the mushrooms with the stem sides up

Add the garlic cloves to pan and cook until lightly
brownedSprinkle with thyme.

Drizzle with 1 tablespoon olive oil and season with sea salt and
blackpepper.

Return to the oven and bake for 5
min.Add the cherry tomatoes to the
pan.

Return to oven and bake until mushrooms become softened, for
5min.

Sprinkle the walnuts over the sweet potatoes and
mushrooms.Serve with the spinach.

Baked Shitake Mushrooms and Kohlrabi

Ingredients

1 pound kohlrabi, halved

2 tablespoons extra virgin olive
oil1/2 pound shitake
mushrooms

8 cloves unpeeled
garlic 3 tablespoons
sesame oil

sea salt and ground black pepper to
taste1/4 pound cherry tomatoes

3 tablespoons toasted cashew
nuts1/4 pound spinach, thinly
sliced

Preheat your oven to 425 degrees
F.Spread the potatoes in a pan

Drizzle with 2 tablespoons of oil and roast for 15 minutes turningonce.

Add the mushrooms with the stem sides up

Add the garlic cloves to pan and cook until lightly browned

Drizzle with 1 tablespoon sesame oil and season with sea salt andblack pepper.

Return to the oven and bake for 5 min.Add the cherry tomatoes to the pan.

Return to oven and bake until mushrooms become softened, for 5min.

Sprinkle the cashew nuts over the kohlrabi and mushrooms.Serve with the spinach.

Baked Purple Yam and Button Mushrooms with Macadamia Nuts

Ingredients

1 pound purple yam, halved

2 tablespoons extra virgin olive oil1/2 pound button mushrooms

8 cloves unpeeled garlic

2 tablespoons chopped fresh thyme1 tablespoon extra-virgin olive oil

sea salt and ground black pepper to taste1/4 pound cherry tomatoes

3 tablespoons toasted macadamia nuts1/4 pound spinach, thinly sliced

Preheat your oven to 425 degrees

F. Spread the purple yam in a pan

Drizzle with 2 tablespoons of olive oil and roast for 15 minutesturning once.

Add the mushrooms with the stem sides up

Add the garlic cloves to pan and cook until lightly brownedSprinkle with thyme.

Drizzle with 1 tablespoon olive oil and season with sea salt and blackpepper.

Return to the oven and bake for 5 min.Add the cherry tomatoes to the pan.

Return to oven and bake until mushrooms become softened, for 5min.

Sprinkle the macadamia nuts over the purple yam and mushrooms.Serve with the spinach.

Baked Button Mushroom and Summer Squash

Ingredients

1 pound summer squash,
halved 2 tablespoons extra
virgin olive oil1/2 pound button
mushrooms

8 cloves unpeeled
garlic2 tsp. cumin

1 tsp. annatto seed

½ tsp. cayenne pepper

1 tablespoon extra-virgin olive oil

sea salt and ground black pepper to
taste1/4 pound cherry tomatoes

3 tablespoons toasted pine
nuts1/4 pound spinach, thinly
sliced

Preheat your oven to 425 degrees F.Spread the summer squash in a pan

Drizzle with 2 tablespoons of olive oil and roast for 15 minutesturning once.

Add the mushrooms with the stem sides up

Add the garlic cloves to pan and cook until lightly brownedSprinkle with cumin , cayenne pepper and annatto seeds.

Drizzle with 1 tablespoon olive oil and season with sea salt and blackpepper.

Return to the oven and bake for 5 min.Add the cherry tomatoes to the pan.

Return to oven and bake until mushrooms become softened, for 5min.

Sprinkle the pine nuts over the summer squash and mushrooms.Serve with the spinach.

Baked Spinach and Winter Squash

Ingredients

1 ½ pounds winter squash, peeled and cut into 1-inch chunks

½ onion, thinly sliced

¼ cup water

½ vegetable stock cube,
crumbled1 tbsp. extra virgin
olive oil

½ tsp cumin

½ tsp ground coriander

½ tsp garam masala

½ tsp hot chili
powderBlack pepper

½ pound fresh spinach, roughly chopped

Put all of the ingredients in a slow cooker except the last
one. Top with handfuls of spinach and stuff the slow
cooker with it.

If you can't fit it all in at once, let the first batch cook first
and add some more spinach.

Cook for 3 or 4 hours on medium until winter squash become
soft. Scrape the sides and serve.

Conclusion

How did you like these delicious vegetarian recipes? If your passion for cooking is strong then I'm sure you will like them.

Unfortunately this book is finished but there will soon be many others, always full of new and delicious vegetarian recipes.

always remember that the best combination to accentuate the benefits of a vegetarian diet is to avoid having a sedentary lifestyle and to do a lot of sport. We send you a big greeting. See you soon.

Lightning Source UK Ltd.
Milton Keynes UK
UKHW032106030521
383075UK00005B/571